This is Now ...
That Was Then

Poems & Prose

by

Patsy Brookshire

Another Touch-My-Heart Production
by
Ruby Rose Truckstop Enterprises

~~~

Cover photos and design by Howard Shippey,
Videographer; Digital Video Designs

Editing by Sunshine Keck, Consultant

Dedication

I dedicate these poems to my dear cousin

Teri McAlary Lund

Skinny little nuisance with the great big heart.

I miss you, kid.

~~~~~

About the Cover of this Book

The MOON setting on Nye Beach in Newport, Oregon, was photographed by Howard Shippey. In this composite, Howard shifted the arch from the Nye Beach entrance to sit on the sand. The photo of Grandma Mabel Brookshire was taken in Long Beach, Washington.

Grandma's clam bag is a gunny sack. That tiny clam in her hand? Surely she returned it to the sea.

About this Second Edition

Questions from readers prompted the addition of information about the cover. The title of the poem "Limited Vision" is now "Bomb Bomb." I included the name of the mailman in "Why I Like Living in a Small Town." Captions have been added or updated on some of the photographs. "Raccoon on the Ceiling" has been edited.

~~~~~

Acknowledgements

Thank you to Sunshine Keck who nudged then pushed me to bring these poems into the sunlight of now. Like a shepherd with flighty sheep, she guided this book to its completion.

Thanks to Howard Shippey who brought my ideas for the cover to life with his design talent, creative photo work and excellent editing. He combined the spirit of my work with the down-to-earth reality of my grandma to turn the cover into a work of art. Well done, Howard, you are a good listener.

How could I not acknowledge and thank my children and friends for support both physical and emotional and even a few financial assists! May I be able to return all in kind.

Let me not forget those old lovers and husbands who provided me with amoré and angst. How lucky for me.

But, gosh, look at my beautiful Grandma Brookshire on the cover in her clamming outfit. She raised 14 children so there were many of us grands. We all knew we were loved and she gave us the best gift ever, time away from our parents. She taught me how to churn butter, pick raspberries, make a quilt on a treadle machine, and when my time came, how to hold my baby in the different ways for burping, sleeping, and loving. Thank you, Grandma.

~~~~~

Also by Patsy Brookshire

Sophie's Kin and Quilt Suspense Series
    Threads
    Scandal at the Willamina Quilt Show

Available as e-books at uncialpress.com

Or in print at Amazon.com and other bookstores

This is Now ...
That Was Then

Poems & Prose

by

Patsy Brookshire

Table of Contents

Talking

Ah, naw,
those crows are talking
about me, again.

Why don't they just shut up
and mind
their own bizness.

Co-Existence
With Design by Bulldozer

Ruby Rose and Loyola Delacorté were
sitting in Ruby's VW van
above the Turnaround,
    just watching the neighborhood change
munching Loy's sour cream potato chips
drinking buttermilk from a carton
anticipating the chocolate candy bar
and
    watching the neighborhood change.
Wondering how much longer
the biker kicking his Harley
in front of the Sandbar
and the polyester lady
going into Cathy's Dress Shop
to check out the threads –
      can co-exist.
Nye Beach should be temporarily
re-named Schizophrenia Village Ruby said.
Where are all the Gilmore people gonna go
Miz Delacorté wondered aloud
and where, they both remembered young Paula asking
are the maids for these fancy condos
going to live
and, she'd thundered,
the fish plant people
and the cooks and the waitresses?
Looking now to the new condo
on the cliff, and
remembering
the fine old house that had withstood

⇒

sea storms, high, hard winds
salt and termites
    but had no defense against the bulldozer
Miz Delacorté and Ruby Rose
wondered
about the poets, and writers, painters,
The Recorders...
Of course
the polyester lady's heart catches
just as skip-a-beat
as does the biker's
the mists will encircle the condos
as thoroughly as the cottages...

But oh,
I just wish,
they both thought out loud
    of the corner on Coast and Olive,
    that,
the bulldozers would pass by
the fine old bushes
of wild roses.

> *Ruby Rose*
> *June, 1984*
> *Nye Beach, Oregon*

Postscript: The Gilmore has been renamed the Sylvia
Beach Hotel.

Proper Dress

The fear is that the
Grand Old Lady of Nye Beach
is gonna turn cutesy on us.

I sure as hell hope
that she doesn't put on
a starched sunbonnet
and a calico dress.
The faded jeans
second-hand shirts
and sturdy shoes
that she has worn
for the last 20 or so years
fit her just fine.

I suppose though,
once the Clas-si-cull Peeple
get through re-juv-i-na-tin her
we'll have to dress down
to go a-visitin'.

High heels and polyester?

Please god don't let
toaster covers
frilly ones
be for sale
on the third floor.

*Re: The renovation of the Gilmore Hotel
into the Sylvia Beach Hotel*

Nye Beach
On the 4th of July
Weekend

Down on the beach tonight
with a fire so bright
and crackers exploding all around

firecrackers and stars

the touri are wild
with ocean air freedom
drunk on sea mist

and wood smoke

roman candles, flares,
rockets and sputteries
that fizzle funny

booms that rock the waves
sand churned by hundreds of feet
hot dogs, marshmallows, sparklers,
hearty laughs in the dark

and it's only the 3rd of July!

Pure

In my calf-length skirt,
ankle socks,
and scarf tied under my chin
I feel like
a fifties movie sweetheart
pure to the core
and innocent.

Walking the beach
below the Turnaround
amidst the tourists
with my pen and blank page book
I am local color.

I feel like Delores Hart
of "Where the Boys Are"
who became a nun.

Hey Moon!

I see you up there
laughing at me
that silly grin
lighting up your
big round face

What's so funny, anyway
you looking so white
and pale
really,
you ought to get out
in the sun
more often.

Blackberry Poem

I try real hard when
that time comes, again, not
to write another
blackberry poem
but
there they are, again,
climbing through my chain fence
filling the gullies all around town
grabbing onto the backsides
of lonely houses
bending in the breeze
and waving their fruit at me
of course there's a bowl
in the fridge
somebody will make pie
and jam
but I just can't resist
getting a few from the vine
for breakfast
for lunch
for dinner, and
for a poem.

Under Cover

A child I work with
told me
he thought
I'd make
a real good bag lady

OH MY GOD!

and here I was, thinking
it didn't show.

Hippie Girls

Oh, where did they go?
Remember the hippie girls
dancing in wide broad green meadows
daisies in their long flying hair
stars painted upon their cheeks
beads swinging on bouncing breasts
scarves wrapped around slim waists
tiny blouses
full skirts printed and patterned
with tie-dyed sunbursts
and spinning in time
to a screaming fiddle
a twanging guitar
their bare feet
and dreamy faces in touch
with the cosmos,
and the blue eyed
flaxen-haired hippie boy
gazing in rapture
at the vision:
his very own hippie girl.

I suspect she's in a tract house
maybe in Colorado
nursing a cold she caught
from the baby
hoping she doesn't give it to
her Scout Troop that's meeting
in her house, this afternoon, but,
I like to think
she's on a farm

⇒

in Oregon or Northern California
milking a goat, her rosy cheek
against the creature's warm flank
she'll make whipped cream
to go with the apple pie
she baked this morning
for the babes
and her hippie boy.
He'll come home in his beat-up
pickup truck, tired from
a hard day in the far field.
They'll eat dinner, pie,
put the babes to bed
and go out to dance in the meadow
under the stars
by the light of a full moon
swaying to the rhythm
of their still deep, still there
Love.

Don't you think that somewhere
the music is still playing?

Dining By The Sea

Toast and coffee by the sea
my fellow diners
do please me

Sand pipers hop
gulls just flap
pelicans glide
without much yap

They're all doing
the same as me
taking breakfast
by the sea.

Teasing Me

The Muse
she tempts me
with her eyes
trailing her fingers
down my spine
until I think
she's going to
lift her skirt, then
she walks away
leaving me
aching.

Seagull Poem With a Twist

I came to the beach today
to get inspiration
to write another
seagull poem
of soaring, dipping
the squawking bird
in all its splendor,
but,
they've been chased from the skies
by different flying beasts.
A yellow one with two red eyes.
A green and red and purple striped one
that flaps against the wind.
An elaborate tri-square
that dips and soars
an airy acrobat
that most seagulls would scorn,
not the fancy flips
but the controlling man
at the kite string end.

Ah, there is one
gray and magnificent
braving the kites
and wind.
He lands.
This is my beach, he struts,
looking for shreds of mussel, clam,
or cheese sandwich leavings.
Our solitary bird stands strong
Feathers ruffling.

⇒

Lo,
the wind picks up
all the kites come down.
Their masters fold their wings
and carry them away.
Solitary Seagull surveys:
mine, all mine.
He flexes his wing muscles.
Ah yes,
a good day for flying.

(The Turnaround, 1984)

Sundaze

Pelicans skim waves
through Sunday
jeweled
ocean haze.

Creeps

Fog
horn blows
lighthouse glows
fog
creeps over the sea.

A Sea Poem

The sea
it's all too easy
to rhyme
with me,
be,
and he
splashing thoughts
of free
about the page
through the lines,
better to watch the dog
running the surf
and forget poetry.

Turnaround Gal

High above the swelling sea
seated on the Turnaround bench
the sun shining,
glinting silver
off the wing tips of soaring gulls
you tell me of life on the prairie
the farms standing alone and spare,
wheat fields and alkali beds surrounding
a life rich
within
those weathered boards

I see you
nearly forty years ago
standing in the Saskatchewan plain
your face rapt with distance
and open space

In my vision I see you
wearing a pink dress
with faded blue flowers
the belt coming undone
barefoot and barelegged, tan
with the deep brown of your eyes
smiling inwardly,
as they still do

⇒

You go into the barn
yes, I can see you there
speaking to the creatures
yes, I can feel them
rubbing soft lips against your hand

I can see why it's called the Turnaround
you say, bringing me back to now
the cars circling brick and concrete
in their brush with the sea

Again it's just you and me
sharing a sunny morning
on the Turnaround bench
above the sea.

For Loyola
from Patty

Again, August

Oh, no it's another seagull,
blackberries are a' ripening,
lone black crow
on the old snag
on the cliff above the beach
poem

He's calling, cawing,
that crow
talking crow talk to a quiet dawn
moving to one of those beach trees
the green boughs bounce
the cool energy of early morning
making him cocky and bossy

His voice echoes through the thin fog

I wonder if crows eat blackberries
and talk to seagulls
?
They're probably too busy
bossing the world around

Yelling at people
who get up early in August
to sit outside and feel the fresh air,
listen to them, watch the seagulls
and write corny poems.

Single Black Crow

Single black crow
walking the white beach
strutting proud
scratching your heels
against the hard sand.

Looking

Midnight and a full moon
all sorts of craziness allowed
on such nights
no rain to dampen the spirits
of wanderers
no fog to falter quick steps
coming, going, looking
into moon shadows
hoping to find a kindred spirit
out walking under the moon
slowly,
looking,
looking.

Where's My Meadow?

I am becoming
a Renoir painting
soft and plump
I need a hat
with cherries on it
so
like a good tart
I can go bouncing
down the street
and
every block or so
break
an old-fashioned heart.

Fast Ducks

Look at those ducks
they move so fast
across
their sky

Going South
on a late August early morn
such rhythm
and single minded purpose,
so fast

I sit
on my porch
the sun new
and warm
on my skin

The kittens sprawl
and scratch their chins

The neighbors
in their shacks
move slowly
babies on their hips
they visit twixt the doors
on a slow search
for coffee
and early morning
communion

Only the ducks
fly fast
spurred by urge

They feel Something

The rest of us
choose
to ignore
the chill sound
of the foghorn,
and the dew,
lingering late
on summer grass.

Why I Like Living in a Small Town

This morning I was sitting on the couch in my jammies even though it is a week day and John is already gone to work, basically because I could. I'm working with an old photo album of my Mom's with the goal of sending a copy of it to my Aunt Nellie (my mother's sister) so she can tell me who the heck some of these people are ("If you want to know anything about any of us you better be asking now") when the mail truck pulled to the front by the mailbox – oh, good, mail, I'm thinking, I'll have to get dressed and go get it later, and then a loud knocking on the door.

I grabbed a big shirt hanging from the back of the chair by the dining table and threw it on, and opened the door in my bare feet, hair going every which way. There's the mailman, but not one I'm used to seeing, holding out my mail and a small Priority box that I take and see is addressed to John Port. My lower nature thought, dang, not for me, followed immediately by better thoughts: oh, good, somebody's sent John a birthday present (he will be 65 this coming Saturday a week from today, the 25th, yes, the day of Sarah's wedding).

Then the mailman says, "David played a good game last night." I just looked at him, rather dumbfounded. I don't know this guy, but he's referring to David, my grandson who played in last night's Newport Cubs Varsity game against Siuslaw's football team, a game that they played in the pouring rain at Newport field with a final score of 38-7. I'll let you figure out who scored what …. It was Dave's first Varsity game and he played from beginning to end with only a couple minutes out.

Finally I say, "Yeah!"

Mailman says, "I think maybe they could've beat 'em," reflectively.

Me, "Oh, I don't know. Those were big guys, farm boys."

MM, "Yeah, Dave and 'G' were hitting 190 pounders." Seeing the question on my face, "My son is number 24." Dave is #7.

"Oh?"

"Did you listen to it on the radio?" he asks.

"I was there."

"Oh." He smiles. We are comrades, both having sat through a game that had several highlights, at least two of them ours, when we got the touchdown and when we got the kick. I was sure that kick would put us ahead of them when our guys got their feet under them because those other guys didn't make all their kicks.... The band, which was right by us (David's mother, Jennifer, and I) and the cheerleaders, directly in front of us, never lost their spirit but leaped and played on with energy, putting their all into every fight song and blast of the horns….

Reminded me of the time when I was 17 and West Linn High was getting creamed something like 33 to 0 by Jefferson High in the State finals but we (WLHS) were happy because we held those bruisers to the lowest spread of their whole year. It was a victory! But I digress.

"G's" dad (G for Giovanni, a check with David tells me) is right, it was a good game, and luckily, not even too cold. The rain kept the air warm, and the bleachers are covered.

My sport's-talk pump is primed. "Those guys are farm boys, used to wrestling cows," I say, ready to talk about the game play by play, but he has his rounds to attend to and he repeats as he is turning away, "They played a good game." He gets in his truck and drives away, having delivered more to me than the mail as I'm left feeling warmed by our shared memory and pride in our boys.

And that other feeling that I like from living in a small town, he knows that the woman at 123 High St. is #7's grandma, and he's confident that I'll be proud of that, as he is of being #24's dad. He's right.

Patsy Brookshire
September 19, 2004

The name of the mailman is Mark Barbers.

Digging Clams by Lantern Light

Allen and I spent the summer of 1955 as usual, picking berries and beans, taking in early July our annual trip with our parents to Long Beach, Washington, to stay in a cabin with Grandma Brookshire to dig, clean, chop, and can razor clams.

~

I'm 13 ½ years old. I hate clams. I hate digging clams. I hate getting up in the middle of the night from my warm bed in our cozy cabin. "Pat, time to get up now. You've wasted enough time lazing in that bed! Your father has the car warmed up, everybody's waiting for you!" Mom's voice penetrates the pillow over my head.

Allen, almost 12, is half asleep in the backseat, his head snugged up against Grandma's comfy shoulder, she in the middle. I open the car door and fall in place on her other side. She lifts her arm so I can lean into her warm softness, her arm around my shoulder, her hand lifting up to pat my head as I continue to moan.

"I don't even like clams." I grumble. "It's cold. I don't see why I couldn't have stayed in bed!"

"Pat!" Mom snaps, "Are you deliberately trying to make everyone miserable?"

"No," I whine.

"Well, then, be quiet and keep your complaints to yourself."

"Yeah," Allen's muffled agreement.

"Oh, brother," I mutter to myself, restraining the urge to reach around Granma and whack him. I sit in sullen silence, thinking, not my fault, wasn't my idea.

Almost asleep again I feel the car move over the sandy gravel road and through the dunes to the long flat beach to drive for almost a mile on the hard, wet sand, past the worm-eaten shipwreck. "Less of it every time we come," says Mom. I open my eyes to see the hull barely visible through the mist in the dark. Eventually, too soon for me, Dad stops, turns off the car and gets out, the closing of the door echoing through me with a painful inevitability.

"Brrr," he laughs, rubbing his hands together, pulling his cap further down around his ears. Allen jumps out the other door, Grandma elbows me out into the cold, following me. I slump against the car, feeling the damp of early morning metal through my jeans, watch my family joyful in the mist. Lord, the worse it is the better they seem to like it. I fold my arms against my chest to trap heat. Grandma goes around to the trunk with Dad to get shovels, buckets, all that dang stuff. He brings out our Coleman lantern, fools with it, strikes a match to the mantle, brings fire and light to the dark seascape.

He hands the lantern to Grandma who takes one of the two buckets, a sack and a shovel that she hands to Allen to carry. She gets her own shovel and the two of them start off across the sand towards the water, their path lit by the lantern. Grandma is wearing her work clothes: an old dress, an old sweater. Her curly white hair sticks out from the blue bandana on her head. She's short and plump but in her old tennis shoes she moves quickly. Dad reaches into the trunk again, brings out our other lantern. I watch him light it while Mom reaches into a box in the trunk, pulls out a wadded-up piece of red material.

"It's dark. And cold," I say, but in spite of myself I start to wake up and get interested in what we are doing. Besides, it's too cold to stand still! I start stomping around.

"Here, Pat," Mom throws me the cloth. I bend my head to put on the bandana and see I'm wearing my new tennies. I sit down on the running board and start undoing the laces.

"Now, what are you doing?" Everything I do irritates her, maybe because she hates getting up so early even more than I do?

"Taking my shoes off. Wrong ones. Miracle I got dressed at all. Getting people out of bed in the middle of the night…."

"Enough! If you want to go barefoot I don't care, just don't whine about it!"

"I just said…!"

"And I said that is enough!" She and Dad gather their gear and start off across the sand, the lantern light swaying as they follow Grandma to the edge of the ocean.

"Ok," I mutter, tired of myself, too. The ridges of the running board are hard against my bottom; the wet of the cold sand on my bare feet wakes me up. There is just enough moonlight to catch the glint of white caps in the distance. The muffled rumble of the waves hitting beach is louder. I'm alone! I grab the remaining shovel and sack, follow the lanterns. We walk quite a ways, this is a way far-out minus tide, the best of the year and the poor clams are just under the sand, their breathing holes exposed to our sharp eyes in the dim light of the lanterns. I stop once in front of a large puddle to roll up my pants legs so I can push through the water – colder still but now I enjoy it, not that I'll ever let them know.

I catch up with Allen and Grandma outlined in a circle of light cast by their lantern on the sand. They're already digging, Grandma's bucket holds salt water she's scooped from the ocean, the bottom is covered with clams – she's the best digger of us all. I don't say much as I join them. I look for the tiny holes in the sand, but only pay attention to the ones that spurt water when I press my toes by them. Ah ha! There's one! I toss the sack aside, turn my back to the ocean to block the clam's escape to the water ..seaward.. slice the narrow shovel blade into the sand. I dig fast, in a furious race with the clam. I'm throwing sand everywhere until I see the suck of a depression at the bottom of the hole .. the clam is digging down as fast as he can. I throw the shovel aside, drop to my knees, plunging my hand as deep as I can into the hole, almost up to my armpits – my fingers scooping up wet, cold, heavy sand until I touch the hard and sharp edge of the clam's shell, and despite pain, hold on, my other hand scooping to get underneath his shell. I get hold, wrap my fingers around his shell, pull him out. A long, flat, brownish shell holds the clam, his digger foot exposed at one end.

"Yea!" He's big enough to keep, his shell cracked where I'd hit him with my shovel. Grandma gives a quick nod but nobody else sees. I don't care, I'm happy. I don't think about the clam, just the contest.

Through the early morning I dig, moving away from the others as daylight comes to let us see each other and the holes without the lanterns, until I've got my limit. I drop the last clam into my sack, its shell *thunks*! against the others – a satisfying sound as I straighten and stretch, smiling to myself. I take a moment to look at the scene: miles and miles of beach on either side of me, seagulls screaming, the ocean roaring in the distance, waves lapping at my toes. I breathe deeply of the salt air, let it all fill my senses – whoops, my feet are sinking in the sand, the minus tide has shrunk. I locate the car and head toward it, angling across the sand pulling off the bandana as I go, the light breeze ruffles my hair. At the car Mom is sitting on the running board, she and Dad and Allen sipping at cups of coffee from Dad's thermos. Grandma's chewing on a cold biscuit.

"I bet I got more than you," Allen challenges as I set my sack down, ready to dump my clams into Grandma's bucket of ocean water where they'll stay alive and clean themselves of sand until we get around to cleaning them later today.

"Bet you didn't!" I said.

"I got 30!" he crowed.

"Huh! That all?" I up-end the sack, gently scooping he contents into the bucket. "I limited."

"36? All by yourself?" He looks in the bucket.

"They'll be good this winter," said Grandma, referring to the clam chowder she'll make from our canning.

"Glad to see you're in a better mood," says Mom. I want to grump a reply but I am happy with the day and looking forward to our morning meal. I have to say just one more thing.

"I'm not eating any of these for breakfast! No clams on my plate!"

"It's ok with me," Dad says as he takes my shovel and empty sack to return to the trunk. "More for me."

"Yeah!" says Allen. "More for me, too! You just don't know what's good" I let him have the last word, looking forward to my eggs fried in bacon grease, and getting back to my bed in our cabin.

~

On the Fourth of July, with hundreds of other families on the beach, each with their own campfire, we set up our fireworks. As soon as the sun sets on the ocean we start lighting firecrackers and rockets, turning peaceful Long Beach into something resembling a war zone. I am 13 ½ - it's glorious.

Patsy Brookshire

Photo of Miz Bella and Prince Charming by Linda Bancke, 2012

Cats and Critters

Pregnant

I sit on my bed
quilt on my lap
typewriter on my knee
a big, fat pregnant cat
curled at the feet of me

She wants to be close
I want her here
we feel better
with each so near

She full of babes
I filled with poems
the moon hanging high
with its fullness nigh

We'll soon all pop
flat we'll be
with poems to read
kitties to feed
and a moon to remember.

Ode to Carl Sandburg

It's a poet's night
with the air orange
and gray
and thick foghorn sounds
drifting through windows
rolling over the backs
    of cats
walking.

Battle of Wills

Muffy sits atop the bookcase.
Her eyes watch as I put kitty Madeline
out the door.
Muffy does not like full moon nights
such as this.
Her retreat to the topmost shelf
protects her, she thinks.
I try to reach her from a chair,
she may be right.
I implore, beseech, scratch like
a mouse, to intrigue.
She glares, I threaten, she twitches
her tail, I retreat.
From my bedroom I hear her jump down,
her way, her choice.
She goes outside; I feel tricked.
This battle of wills was a draw.

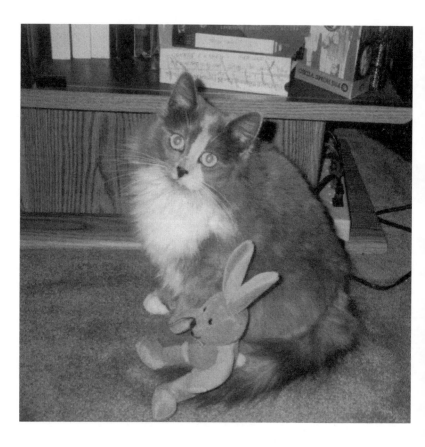

Miz Streak
Christmas, 2003

Jealousy

Kitty, jealous cat
jealous of a pen
the paper too
put down pen
Kitty goes away
pick it up again
Kitty's back to play.

Peaceable Kingdom,
Raccoon on the Ceiling

Summer is really here on the Central Oregon Coast - how do I know in this land of mist and fog? Because I changed the sheets yesterday, finally giving up the flannel to the cool of cotton.

Mother raccoon brought her three babies by to scarf up the birdseed that had fallen to the ground below the feeder. Their humped little bodies are almost as large as hers, but not quite, and they do kid stuff, running around looking at this and that, getting into sibling squabbles. *He's getting more seed than me!* Mom cuffed them when it became more than she could bear, like a mother reaching around to the backseat on a long trip, a flip of her hand/paw just connecting to restore some discipline.

Eventually the kids tire of birdseed on the ground, *obviously these are the leftovers,* and begin to look up at the full feeder suspended from a bushy branch, seeing the baffle that keeps them from climbing the pole. *That branch is hanging oh-so-close to the top of the feeder. Could we?* Two of them run to the tree, scaling the bark like it was a ladder, to stop at that particular branch. Yes, they are smart early on. Smarter mom didn't bother. One of the other kits followed and as they climbed the tree I was sharply reminded of an experience a few days ago, a scary one between a scruffy, canny adult raccoon and me.

Smart kitty Prince Charming had opened the back door (he can do that if it is left the tiniest bit unsecured), and as usual, hadn't closed it behind him. Mr. Scruffy Raccoon knew that

65

the good stuff, the bowl of cat food, is just inside the door with a convenient bowl of water beside it. Plus, and this is the real score, a large bag of cat food sitting there unprotected.

John and I were at the end of our afternoon nap when the low growl of a cat woke me. Getting up, I followed the sound downstairs where I saw Prince on the back of the living room couch, looking at the open door and a raccoon feeding from a hole in the bottom of the bag that he'd gnawed open.

All raccoons are "Rocky" to me. I shouted, "Get out Rocky!" which startled him, not to turn around and run out the door, but towards me. This wasn't what he meant at all so he started to turn back towards the door but he was already in the living room and got confused. Meanwhile Prince was watching. *Let the striped-tail-buzzard have the food, my people will give me more.*

In his confusion Rocky was spurred to higher anxiety by my screaming, plus the moaning from John upstairs, that sounded like, "What going on?"

Rocky ran past me. Lordy be, as I yelled louder "Get out of the house!" he jumped onto the dining table and at increased volume from me, "No! Get off the table!" he leaped onto the front windowsill, clinging to the wood frame separating the windows, and started scrambling up it like the kits do on the tree trunk. He was now above me, over my head. "No! No!"

Meanwhile, John's moans turned into clearer speech, "What the heck is going on?"

Rocky reached the ceiling beam that runs the length of the living room and began an upside down traverse across it. Raccoon overhead. I grabbed a broom and swiped at him.

Seeing a spot between me and the open door, he dropped from the ceiling to the floor; he was very close to my bare feet. Shouting, I chased him with the broom. He scrambled, his claws scritching on the wood floor. He ran out the back door.

John came down the stairs saying, "I told you not to leave the door open unless you want raccoons in the house." He closed the door.

Hmmmm. So helpful.

Now, with my eyes on the kits in the tree, I wonder if they will climb down the branch. They do the math and realize the inches separating the branch from the feeder are too many. Eventually, they all ramble away.

Summer is definitely here, with cotton sheets, raccoon babies, and the garden coming on with peas, beans, tomatoes and zucchini.

July 17, 2012

Love Story of a Bay and a Gull

Every morning the bay orchestra starts with a light show, the premiere being held in the harbor, the scene being different with the vantage spot from which you choose to watch.

Into the deep blue of pre-dawn comes a subtle black-ink pen tracing rigging, a mast, the bridges of ships pale through the morning fog. Look away for the space of a breath, look back; everything is outlined in soft pink.

Across this lavender light glides a seagull, landing heels down on the bay. His rump registers the cold water, he lets out a squawk and the music begins, the morning symphony of the harbor.

Echoing about the Bayfront a chorus of crows in the trees surrounding the bay add their hungry grackling music. A sea lion barks a hello to the dawn that can be heard clear uptown. He dives, comes up with a thrashing fish clamped tight in his jaws and the gulls descend on him.

Squalling their greed they swoop low to catch pieces torn loose in the battle. Snarling at these early birds with his fiercest face he snaps his head at them and plunges under the water again, leaving the gulls to flap about, screaming at each other.

A graceful counterpoint is made by a cormorant riding the small waves taking her breakfast in smooth dips. This lady of the bay sits serenely at table with these raucous fellows, ducking muffled burps to her bosom.

At the edge now of true day there is a hush, the air expectant with the question every Newporter wakes with:

Please, God, the sun? Even gulls temporarily cease their squalling. They line the jetties, sit on old pilings, and squat on the dock. All face east.

The quiet deepens.

Mist dusting gray on the far shore begins a slow rise through the trees. It takes with it the pink, turning everything to a sudden life-worth-living moment. Awe.

Ah, Thank You. Glowing, warming, red through the trees, the finale. The sun. The light show of dawn is over; another day begins in Newport.

The harbor fog horn sounds its final note, mixing with the, again, screeching birds and the faint hum of the wily Winnebago slowly making its way down Bay Boulevard … enjoy.

~~~

Originally published in a Newport paper, the *Gilmore Gazette*, in my column "Local Color" by Pat Brookshire. Used by permission. The *Gilmore Gazette* was published in the 1970's and 1980's out of the Gilmore Hotel by Ed Cameron. Ed is the author of *Gilmore by the Sea, A Graphic Novel*.

That Was
Then

Patsy Brookshire, Jennifer (Chaney) Morley,
Greg Chaney, Clarence Brookshire

Greg's graduation in Fairbanks, Alaska

May, 1987

The Moment

The moment
A dot of time:
Myself on the middle
of the stairs   up
towards Bob sleeping
in our bed   down
towards Gregor asleep
in his bed   and
Jennifer freshly asleep
in her crib
sighing baby milk breath
taken from my breasts
only moments ago
a dot in time ...

The calendar says
it was seventeen years ago
but my mind says
        Ah-h   no,
it was but a moment ago.

October 23, 1982

Bomb Bomb

We sat there at the kitchen table
He and I.
He drew diagrams and figured figures
fancy formulas never meant for
the baby to drink.
Dark came through our homemade curtains.
We flipped on a light
and he talked on.
I listened, trying to understand
just how
if we wanted to
and had some plutonium
or some uranium
perhaps both, I'm not sure now,
we could build a bomb right here
on this table.
A Kitchen Bomb.

He was a rather gentle man,
caring of people, our children, and me.
A student of physics, and chemistry,
not a revolutionary.
I listened closely, that was my way.
With one ear to him,
the other open to the babies, upstairs.
It, he, fascinated me.

$\Rightarrow$

I listened and watched as
he covered the backs of
old computer paper with drawings,
moving the salt and pepper shakers,
the butter plate, our coffee cups, around.
My salt shaker a neutron,
the pepper, a proton,
here and there an ion
everywhere a bomb bomb.

I wonder if he misses my
sense of humor.
I was much too simple for him.

For about five minutes there
in my very own late night kitchen
I knew how to build a bomb,
A Big One
capable of blowing us all to
shadows on a wall . . .
then I lost it.
I hadn't the vision.
The table turned into a place to knead bread
and eat chicken rice (with stars) soup.

I do know we'd be better off
if we had no bombs and more bread.

Originally titled: "Limited Vision"

Wish I Was Home

A pleasant talk with dad
today, on the phone
The gardens about all in
wish I was home

Corn cut down
stalks carried away
For some cows to eat
'long with their hay

Tomatoes all canned
sealed up tight
Zucchini is in
tastes just right

Apples and pears,
blackberries done
Juices a' drippin'
Missed the fun

He's done some fishing
caught a few
Other'n that
not much new

Stopped by the bridge
where we used to buy ice cream
Watched the fish below
of past days did dream

⇒

Sometimes my breath
near stops,
a longing pain
For those seemingly
simpler days
of my youth to feel again

Mom's gone now
with her fun grin, so silly
The dirt roads we traveled
now paved, less hilly

The miles we traveled
in distance and mind
Cannot be re-captured
nor re-done in kind

For then and today
I am thankful
Phone calls and mail
worth more than a bank-full

Talked with Dad
today, on the phone
For just a while,
a touch
a kiss, a smile,
Wish I was home.

Winter

Old,
    and cold,
two words that rhyme
so well with mold

Reminding one of Oregon
    window sills

Touching off a memory
    of outrageous
      heating bills

And a little girl's sniffles

From being too bold
playing in the cold
wearing a coat
one brother old

And just laughing
at that ol' window sill mold.

Susi

Susi is my doll baby.
She's been with me forty years
rescued from a torn-down house
by a laborer and given to me.
My baby.
She lives in my room.

Susi gets independent and sits up
all night on the chest
I've also seen her lazy, lying
on a pile of dirty clothes
basking in the human smoky smell
of her mother.

She's old, for a doll baby.
Her sewn-on feet
are nearly worn off.
Her hair is all gone
it was long and blond.
Her eyes are still blue
but not as sharp as they used to be.
That's why some nights she has to
snuggle close and feel her mother.
Just making sure.
Susi.

The Blink of an Eye

I watched, howling, with closed eyes
as my mother turned into gold sparkles
surrounded by lavender.
Is she the stars or the sky
I don't know. She is
iridescent gold twinkling like white stars
in a black black night.

I watched, unbelieving, as a caterpillar
drew a coat of white silk firmly over his body
and prepared to die, wearing a
shroud of silken threads hanging
from a stick taped onto my windowsill.

My mother's spirit, body no more
sped towards the circle that
opened as she drew near
I tried to pull her back.
Selfish. Don't go. Through.
The circle closed. She on the other side.
I can't open it. I try.

The caterpillar dies. I can see
the black soup mass inside.
I should throw it away. Bury it.
It hangs untended a few more days,
turns luminous green
dots of true gold form a line
against the green, an outline of wings
black and yellow press
inside the thin canvas.

⇒

And I watch.

The circle is closed tight. Gold
sparkles blink silently, go out.
She is gone. I am alone,
She transforms into joy.

I turn my eyes from the cocoon
for a long moment,
busy with my life, and look back,
alerted by movement.
The butterfly, Monarch, hangs,
alive,
in my kitchen, pulsing and wet.
I gasp, transform into joy.

They go. They tell me nothing
of their journey. Enough
that I get to
watch.

Patsy
Oct. 28, 1987
Newport, Oregon

I Walked On

I touched the air tonight
it lay cupped in my palm
then floated away
mingling with other bits of air
taking on moisture
turning grey

I walked on
the sound of the fog horn
moaning through my ears

I walked on
the grains of sand
sliding beneath my feet
keeping me from falling
to the middle of the earth

I walked on
towards the sea
into the water, salt
flowing into my mouth
all the pores of my body open
nibbled at by little fish
with big eyes

I walked on
coming up out of the sea
into a land where
nobody knew my name
it was raining there
the people rushed
by with bowed heads   ⇒

85

I walked on
through forests
and desert oceans of heat

I walked on
to come upon a land
stranger still
filled with people who
looked like me and
spoke my language
yet moved too quickly to touch
it was noisy
with radios and TVs and
cars that raced by

I walked on
coming at last
to a street of fog
I held again the cool grey
in my open hand

I am the fog
I am the sea
I am the earth
and the cars rushing by
wanting more
I rise to the sky
wanting
to be a star.

Kerryann Brookshire flanked by her parents Catherine
Buchholz Brookshire Ehle and Allen Brookshire

University of Oregon Graduation

Aug. 10, 1991

Kerryann

I remember when
your mommy and daddy
first presented you to me,
let me hold you.
You couldn't smile yet
but it was there,
behind your eyes that said,
"Hi! I'm Kerryann! I'm so glad
to be here. Isn't this fun!"

You looked like a moonbaby to me,
special,
all big eyes and no hair,
glowing with life,
cool with secrets
from another sphere,
happy to be here,
like an excited traveler
who just can't wait
to see what's next.

I hesitate to tell you
my moonbaby impression
for fear you will think
I thought you weird,
I told no one at the time
for that very reason.
But, you see,
I've always loved the moon,
constant, yet ever changing.

⇒

As you've grown you have
incorporated the sun
into your spirit,
brightening the air
and lives around you.

I took you to the park
when you were three or four,
and all the kids
wanted to play with you.

Watching you play marbles
with Grandma Brookshire
is one of my highlight memories
of you both, a true match!

You've developed into a
beautiful young woman
with wondrous hair
and a glorious smile,
backed by a bright mind
and a generous spirit.

You still carry that aura
that says, "Hi! I'm so glad
to be here. Isn't this fun!"
Well, yes dear, most of the time,
it is. And I am so glad
you're here, too, sharing this
earth time with me.

Moonbaby, sunlit woman,
may all the stars be yours.

> *Love,*
> *Aunt Pat*

Brookshire Family

Left to right: Mabel (York) Brookshire (Grandma); William Brookshire (Grandpa); Ernie Brookshire (one of Patsy's uncles); Helen (Lackey) Brookshire (Patsy's mom); Clarence Brookshire (Patsy's dad); Allen Brookshire (Patsy's brother); Patsy.

Photo was most likely taken in 1945 at Patsy's parents' farm in Beavercreek, Oregon (near Oregon City).

Selling The Family Home

Washing the cupboard doors
for the last time
while listening to 40's records
on the old console stereo

Looking at the clean square place
on the wall
where my High School graduation
picture has hung
I haven't recognized that young lady
for years

Though I remember
sitting still and tall
for the camera
with no comprehension
that I was being frozen in time.

I look today
at my father's hands
veined and wrinkled
he takes the plastic flowers
from the kitchen window
flowers Mother gathered years ago
he so gently washes dust and
grimy wood smoke into the kitchen sink.
They shine as if picked only yesterday.

⇒

Tomorrow we will search
under the lilac bush
for shoots to dig up
and take with us

We'll leave the roses
and the shade
under the old apple tree

I don't like
putting all these memories
into boxes.

Hugs

If tiny granddaughters
only knew
how
their running-to-Grandma
hugs
grab her heart,
they'd never stop.

Gramma Pat

To Amber, 14 months old
To Krysta little soft sweetie
To David running boy
To Connor the thinker
  and
All the grandchildren in the world.

The Face

We call her The Face
'cause she's so cute
when she gets mad
she scrunches it up
in a tight little bundle
she's not very humble
to force us to do
just what she wants
it does make us laugh
though we try so hard not to
then she gets happy
her smile spreads about
it covers her face
it lights up the room
(go 'way, gloom)
it covers the wall
it spreads to the ceiling
she gives to us all
such a good feeling

We love The Face
reflecting the
irrepressible Amber
deep within.

Gramma Pat

Crow Breakfast

The hungry crow
flew, black and slow
over the cornfield
she did go

Looking for food
was her mood
just one big bite
would be good

In the field
protecting the yield
stood a man
a straw corn-shield

That old straw man
a tattered sham
scared her not
she had a plan

She'd glide right by
with a watchful eye
he'd only hear
a satisfied sigh

down for the bite
like a spiraling kite
that black crow flew
the wind was right

the air was hot
her aim was not
but she got so close
shook up the corn lot

The man did hear
and feel her near
those flapping wings
he ignored her scornful leer

The wind it blew
right on his shoe
he started dancing
was all she knew

Crow moved right smart
with a pounding heart
she didn't much like
this scary part

He shook his head
She darted in dread
But snagged a kernel
This dance she led

Her mouth was full
from one good pull
with a raggy hand
he waved farewell

Breakfast in the
cornfield
          never dull!

Blue

She calls it "feeling blue"
I think she's just plain sad
I hate to see her
feeling so damned bad

Things haven't worked out
quite the way they should
the way we'd been told they would
if we just was "good"

Marrying a "good man"
you know all the rest
have the babies
pass the "goodness" test

Shine the golden ring
at least once a week
make sure he is happy
be always kind and sweet

On Mother's Day be grateful
on Father's scrape just a bit
if it wasn't for his presence
your life would be a pit

I don't like to see her sad
'cause I feel it too
we couldn't be good as gold
it never did .. ring .. true

I'd like to feel some pity
for our deserted men
but it just ain't in me
I can't be false to 'then'.

The Yellows

In the big city
on the jive streets
ya get the blues

In small town world USA
we jest get the yellows
feeling pale
like a rained-on sunset
shot through
with streaks of grey
feeling kinda dull
wondering what's gonna happen next,
if anything…

Feeling blue
with
The Yellows.

"All American"

His Blackness looming large
against my oh so Whiteness
I asked him if he minded
if I sat there, beside him.
He shifted ever so slightly
closer to the window in
bus-rider politeness and said
No, sit down.
It was not yet dark
the farm hill scenery
of Nebraska was commented on
until we could get to his rage
of Vietnam Vet insulted,
his pride stomped on, over, around.
We talked kids, wives, husbands, drugs never
to be used again, and Vietnam.
I put forth my theory of Roy Rogers childhoods
shattered on the bloody fields of Nam –
He politely and partially agreed.
He spoke of the shock and
the treacherous kids.
The lack of color
of who was behind
and who was in front
on a night oh so dark jungle search.
We were the same age
knew each other through
shared same time history
though his Blackness
and my Whiteness
his maleness and my femaleness
could have separated us.   ⇒

He'd been on the streets
he'd been in the jungles
he'd fallen in love
and stopped, he said,
but I don't believe him,
the madness within, through love.
Tamed, by love. Of a Good Woman.
As natural as apples and crust
we blended into a late night
cross country All American Pie.
Telling truths to each other.
Morals. Kids. Feelings. Teaching.
God. Country. Color. All American
kind of talk. Without the music
background in our ride
across the country.
We ate together in an All
American fast food buffet.
We slept beside each other on an All
American bus.
We clung together emotionally
in the late night brightness of the
All American Bus Terminal
white tile floors
Go Greyhound on the walls
I see his two little girls
that loving wife
as if they were my own.
We parted in the basement
of the Chicago terminal
his face one last look at mine
before he turned and went
up the stairs.   ⇒

I'm glad we said no formal Goodbye;
I wish I'd kissed his heart
put his hand on mine.
Damned if I can remember
his name.
And equally damned
If I ever forget
His story.

1987 Cross country bus trip
From Newport, OR. to
Detroit, D.C. and back.

Nov. 29, 1987
Nye Beach

If I Had No More Traveling To Do

If I had no more traveling to do
I could sit at ease
on a wooden step
watch my backyard garden bloom
but I hear the call of the loon
across a misty lake
and the horn
across a foggy bay
I feel the sun of an Arizona afternoon
upon my bones too cool
I see the orange of a harvest moon
rising somewhere I have never been

If I had no more traveling to do
I could with ease
weed the flower patch out front
instead of listening for the flying geese
feeling the road under wheels
thinking of a rabbit track
in a Canadian woods
a too young girl
in a Mexican bar, sitting beneath
a velvet Christ

⇒

If I had no more traveling to do
I would not be imagining the China Wall
at dawn
or remembering the Mogollon Rim
in storm with lightning crackling
beneath my feet
I would not be wanting to hear
corn grow in Iowa in hot hot summer
or to sit in an apple orchard in Yakima
letting blossoms fall upon me

The world waits for me
to come and see
if I could only ignore the call
of the whippoorwill
through a Great Lakes woods,
I would sit and tend my garden
        forgetting the Northern Lights
        dancing beneath an Alaskan sky
if only
I had no more traveling to do.

Canning Peaches on Harvest Moon

Had a call today from niece Amanda in Portland, she and husband Michael are canning pears. They canned peaches yesterday. Boy, does that bring back memories. Daughter Jennifer asked me several years ago, when her (now grown) kids were little, did I know how to can peaches? No, I said, thinking, sure, I canned a million of 'em but Mom was in charge of that production, I, with Allen and Dad, just went along.

Then my mind recalled the process (like a video) from the beginning, with bringing up the dusty canning jars from the basement to wash in our kitchen's white enamel double sink. Very hot water, by hand. Jars dried on towels while we took fuzzy peaches from the wooden lugs (boxes) where we'd put them when we picked them the day before in Carver, or Damascus (or bought, we sometimes did that). Putting them in cool water on the stove to take out as soon as the water started to boil, and slipping off the skins. Cutting each and every peach in half to get the pit out, by now the juice is running into my armpit, the room is getting hotter than outside, (and that's hot). Everything is hot and sticky. Cutting each peach in even slices, perfectly evenly, mind you, to slip into the warm jars.

Making sugar and hot water syrup, setting a funnel on top of each jar and pouring the syrup into the jar. Putting on the flat lids, perfectly even, screwing down the top. Filling the metal carrier with, was it six? of the filled jars, lifting the whole batch into the blue speckled canner that was half full of hot water,

111

boiling them for ten? minutes, lifting the hot carrier by the metal handles, with hot pads, from the boiling water and setting it to cool on the counter. Lifting the jars from the carrier with the special tool that attached to the neck of the jar, setting them on the dry towel on the counter. Making sure of no draft, not too cool too quick or the hot jars might break. Listening and counting the pops of the lids as they sealed. Doing it all day, and the next day, too. Peaches, pears, tomatoes, green beans, prunes, etc. Some the hot water bath method, some things in the pressure cooker, a nervous procedure for Mom as she was afraid it would explode; we were nervous, too. Never did. Basement shelves full of precious winter food.

Jen and I drove the kids to Sherwood to a peach orchard, gathered fresh, sweet, juicy peaches from the ground ("Mind the bees, kids"), brought them back to their home in Newport, Jen worried that we'd not gathered enough peaches. Two hours there, two hours back. Worked late into the night canning the lovelies. Those just might be the best canned peaches I've ever eaten. Remember, Jen?

Patsy Brookshire
September 14, 2011

Mr. and Mrs. Port at the Peaceable Kingdom
John Port and Patsy Brookshire

Only Him, Not Her

José and Maria were dancing down
at The Hall in the old mining town.
They swirled and they dipped,
he bowed, she curtsied.
He pulled her to him,
they swayed cheek to cheek.
The people spread out to watch
his gray hair, workworn clothes,
devoted loving attention
to his absent partner;
They could only see him, not her.

He took her to their table,
Pulled out her chair,
Lifted her hair from
off her neck to cool her,
brought her lemonade
in a paper cup.
They made small conversation
such as couples do after dancing,
laughing lightly while
fanning themselves.
No one sat down to chat;
They could only see him, not her.

I watched this solitary dance in
Globe, Arizona. 1979

True Blue

The man had blue eyes
The 1st one
The 2nd one
The 3rd one too
He winked at me
He smiled at me
He flashed the cutest grin
Now what could
a girl like me do ..
I let him come on in.
He flirted and romanced me
He brought me cherry brandy
He told me silly jokes
he said we'd last forever
I was The Only One
I believed all three of these folks ..
They all left town
as blue-eyed men are wont to do
they all cried
said they didn't want to
they left just the same ..
My crying's done
'cause here's another one
he's knocking at my door
flashing ice, and fire, electric blue
Aw, this one I just know
this one, he will be true!

Feeding

The making of breakfast
for a hungry man
has many feelings.
If the man be son
it's pleasure
to feed, to nourish.
If the man be father
it's pleasure
to feed, to please.
If the man be husband
it's pleasure
To feed, to satisfy duty.
If the man be lover
it's pleasure
to feed, to strengthen,
just barely
enough
so he will remember the taste
and come back for more.
The breaking of egg
frying of bacon
toasting of bread
surpasses all gifts
I can give
feeling to be poetry
in motion
each movement
smooth and fluid
coming from a certainty
of rightness
full-feeling the want
to be needed, the want   ⇒

to care for, the want
to give love, health,
pleasure
so that you will be here,
again tomorrow
hungry again,
for me.

The Man in the Moon is My Lover Tonight

I go walking
through the dark woods
with only a glimmer of light
from above
my heart is beating fast,
anticipating
the man in the moon
who is my lover tonight

Tendrils of vine
clinging to my waist
I find our meadow
bare myself to the night,
and wait

Towering firs a misty haze
seen through closed eyes
vigil on a bed of moss
a webbed coverlet of dew

I lie in silence
awaiting his kiss
on my lips ..
a glow
I open my eyes

⇒

121

His touch is soft and
slowly mounts my passion
higher and higher as he
climbs the sky
caressing my thighs
while I look
from the forest floor
into his eyes

The man in the moon
is my lover tonight

Reaching the zenith
of the sky I gasp
bursting into flame
from the heat
of his cool touch

He blinks behind a cloud
as I cascade into peace
his warm seed deep
within me, I sleep

Dreaming of the man
the man in the moon
who was
my lover tonight.

Desperado Prints

I send you away
let you go out the door
you carry my prints all over
your neck, your mouth
I grab the shirt you left
some time ago
wrap myself in you
to keep the passion warm.

Desperado Thief

Have you ever had a man
steal your heart,
only to find
that he wants your car,
too?

The Perfect Man

knows how to give a massage
and likes to eat breakfast out
he loves to chop wood
and let me build the fire,
is 4 to 5 inches taller than me
and takes a strong lead when we dance
best of all the perfect man
thinks I have cute legs
and he tells me so.

The Eyes Have It

It's always the eyes
the ones that shine
with just that bit
of sin
that glow with the grin
that light up when
a pretty girl
comes in
yeah,
it's always
the eyes that
do me in.

You Had to 'av Been There...

It was another hot night
in December
the moon being so white
warmed my loins.

3:00 a.m. in Newport

Being in Sambo's so
late at night
makes me feel like
I'm traveling.

Crosswords Puzzle

"The sooner you get
out of my life," she said,
the happier I'll be!"

"No happier than me,
and you can count on it!"
he said.

They walked on past my
cabin, together.

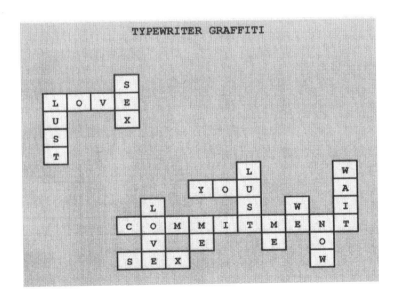

Tired

The wild horse of time
is running away with me
dashing so fast about the streets,
my knees are tiring from holding on.

Holding...

Jet planes and I
have two things in common,
fast travel across vast spaces
only to circle
in a long holding pattern
before landing.

Anniversary Blues

The moon hangs sliced orange
in the sky.
Misty air catches on the porch web.
Down on the beach the tips
    of waves
are doing a salty intercourse with
    the sand
and I know,
I just know,
that somewhere people are
    dancing to a spicy
    rock n' roll beat
        while you sleep.

I Sure Would Like

to have a new boyfriend
someone I can talk with
take a long walk on the beach with
he'd sit around campfires
    with me
in the grocery store he'd hold hands
    with me
I'd go to the café in the mornings
have coffee with him
he wouldn't have to do anything exotic
like take me to Greece
or buy me rubies at hundreds
of dollars apiece
just let me cook him bacon and eggs
    now and then
go for a ride with me in the country
    now and then

    . . .

maybe if I'm a good girl
Santa will bring me one for Christmas

    . . .

or bring the old one back.

Ruby Rose

Aunt Nellie Brookshire and Cricket in
Gladstone, Oregon, late 1940's

142

The Week of Incredible Snow

In the late 40's in Gladstone, Oregon, when I was a little girl, about eight, it was winter and it started to snow. It snowed so that the whole world was white and piled up with it. Magical. I'd never seen anything like it. Mother went out with a broom and knocked the heavy snow off the roses, the lilac and sumac trees. The weight was breaking off limbs; it made her cry. She, being from Wyoming and my dad from Montana, was not as enamored of the snow as my seven-year-old brother, Allen, and me, but even they were amazed at the enchantment. Her sister Nellie was visiting. Mom took a photo of Aunt Nellie and our collie dog Cricket with his front feet on Aunt Nellie. To complete a perfect day Mother made bread. Nothing matches the aroma that fills the house when bread is baking. After she took it out of the oven she cut slices for us that we buttered and ate. Yeasty bread, warm tummies, home.

Two more memorable things happened that week of incredible snow. The first: I heard a knock on the door and opened it. No one there. I heard a muffled voice, "Hello," and looked down to see a very small girl on our porch. The child was a stranger to me, completely wrapped with coat, mittens and a scarf around her neck. Big boots. Her hat nearly covered her face but I could see that she was probably about four years old, maybe five. "Who are you?" I asked.

"I'm Leila Jo Repaskeay and I just moved in down the street. Can you come out and play?" The littlest girl ever, with that big name. I've spelled her name phonically: Re-pass-key-a. We welcomed her into our neighborhood gang of kids.

It was a week of sledding and building a snowman, but best of all was the walk I took with my dad. The street had not yet been snowplowed so the whole world was deep in white drifts. I wore my yellow rain boots and thick socks. People out but no cars. Everything so white, so quiet. We needed groceries so Dad and I walked the six long blocks downtown admiring and comparing other snowmen to ours, talking with neighbors about the snow, the cold, the weather, like people do. Ray's Market, the only grocery in town, was (and still is), on the corner of the main street. The soda fountain was a couple stores down but it was too cold for a fountain drink, and the candy store was across the street but we needed groceries, so, no stopping there. Our purchases made we walked those long six blocks home, me feeling like a very special girl to be walking alone with Daddy. When we arrived home, Mom toasted us a couple more pieces of bread. With a bit of strawberry jelly that she'd made in the summer, the day ended just right.

All that in a piece of bread. As an adult when I see a flake of snow my bread baking gene, as John says, gets activated. Now you know why when it snowed yesterday I pulled out the greasy card from my old recipe box and set the yeast to rising in a small bowl of warm water with sugar. When done it tasted just as good as it did when I was that child in a magical land. Almost.

January 16, 2012

Home Made Bread

Oven: 400° F. 15 min.　　　　　Yield: 2 loaves.
　　　350° F. 30 min.

1 cake yeast　　　　　　　Shortening, half of 1/3 cup
1/8 cup lukewarm water　　1 T. sugar
1/2 teaspoon sugar　　　　1 T. salt
　　　　　　　　　　　　　1 cup scalded (hot) milk
　　　　　　　　　　　　　Water, half of 3/4 cup

5 – 6 cups sifted flour

*Combine yeast mix, set in warm place. Let rise until light and spongy. Approx. 15 min.

*Combine Shortening, sugar, salt, milk. When shortening is melted add cold water. Cool until lukewarm. Add yeast. Fold in until well mixed.

*Add flour as it can be stirred in above mixture. Turn out onto floured board or table. Knead until smooth and satiny. Put in large bowl – brush top with shortening. Cover with towel. Let rise until double in bulk (2 hours). Punch down. Separate half, shape for pans. Let rise again in pans. (1 hour).

*Bake. Butter. Eat.

A Safe Place

It's 1946, Gladstone, Oregon, a town of over 2000 people. I have a younger brother and parents. I'm four years old, the new kid on the block and have met a girl my age, down the street, Dorothy. She becomes my first, and lifelong Best Friend. Her mother, Mrs. V., becomes my first Ideal Mother.

In my time in Gladstone Mrs. V. and Mr. V. moved from a house down the street from me to one street over. Dorothy would eventually have three younger brothers and a sister. The house they lived in when I first moved there was a typical 30's, 40's style house. One story, 3 bedrooms, bathroom, living room and small kitchen with dining area attached. White clapboard siding. Unusual was a gas pump in the back yard. Beside it was a heavy duty pickup, and a big yellow Caterpillar tractor. Mr. V. built roads. There was a long block between our homes.

Lavern lived at the top of the block where Dorothy and I sat with Lavern on the front lawn and sang *The Tennessee Waltz*.

Two houses down was Leila Jo R., a little girl who appeared on my doorstep one snowbound day, wrapped like a mummy, asking if she could come in and play. Three houses down lived David, the boy with deaf parents – as he left his house he signed to his mother in the doorway, while hollering to us as he joined our neighborhood kid gang. Across that street cater-cornered from Dorothy was Billy Bell. Billy and his mother lived with his grandparents. Father dead in the war? Always a mystery. They had the truly classic two-story white house with a big backyard and a cherry tree in front. He was rich, that we knew because he drove up and down the sidewalk in his car. I don't remember, was it electric, battery driven, or

147

did he pedal it? I never drove it. Probably as a girl that wouldn't have even been thought of.

My mother drove a car but, like many of our friends' mothers, Mrs. V. didn't. To do her local shopping she used a stroller that carried both a child and a basket for groceries. To go to Oregon City or Portland she took the streetcar. As often as not we all walked with her when she went to Ray's Market, four or five blocks down the street to Gladstone's shopping and business area of one street, several blocks long. Grocery store, drug store with a fountain counter, businesses in between, with a tavern at one end, near the butcher and locker store, where we kept our frozen meat in our rented locker. A bakery and a café. Across from Ray's was a 'five and dime' with a full, glass-fronted, candy counter. City Hall had steps to the business area and a library through a door you entered from the side. Dorothy and I read just about every book in that library.

Back at Dorothy's house her bedroom had a bookcase with her own books in it. I vowed to myself to someday have my own bookcase. Dorothy's room had curtains and a bedspread for a girl, it wasn't a room for boys. Dorothy designed, and we cut out, paper dolls, made up stories and had the dolls act them out. We played her records, harmonizing *Cool Water* with the Sons of the Pioneers, and one memorable day when Mrs. V. had gone somewhere without us, made fudge. It became so thick that we couldn't even scrape it out of the pan and so threw the whole shebang into the garbage can at the side of their house. Denied for forty years that we knew anything about where that pan might have gone.

Dorothy's mother was sweet. She was round and gentle, and let us do about anything that we came up with. She was an excellent housekeeper who wore, as did all the mothers, a dress with full apron. Nearly a uniform. She wore her hair rolled back into soft curls on both sides. There was a sweet light in her eyes. When they built and moved to the new place, a block over, it was high stepping. The gas pump moved with them. A modern ranch house, with three low steps to the front door and a brick-lined flowerbed beside it. You stepped into a living room with a fireplace. At Christmas Mrs. V. hung stockings from the mantle and Santa filled the socks. Because of my mother's religion for those years, we didn't do that at our house. One year Santa left Dorothy a wristwatch in her stocking. I probably remember that more than she does. When we came home from school Mrs. V. was always there. The house was clean, orderly, neat, smelling of just-baked cookies. They had a coffee table. That place was like a Hallmark card.

It was her domain. A radio sat near the end of her kitchen counter. While she worked she listened to the soap operas *Dr. Kildare*, or *Ma Perkins*. It seemed to me a ladylike and sophisticated thing to do, to be entertained while you worked.

If Dorothy did something wrong Mrs. V. would say, in her soft voice, "Now, Dorothy, you don't do that." A rebuke by Mrs. V. was serious. My own mother was a loving person, but she had flashes of anger that never happened with Mrs. V. It was a safe place. She listened to us. Did we entertain her, or was she just being polite – never to know. She didn't tell us her thoughts.

When I call up my picture of the early Mrs. V. I see her at the handle of the baby stroller with at least one baby and a toddler in it, and us on our way downtown. There we might catch the streetcar where we would ride with her the couple miles to Oregon City, or, as I remember doing at least once, going the other way to the end of the line which in downtown Portland. On the way there and back the streetcar stopped at Oaks Amusement Park. Maybe we went roller skating in the rink there? The streetcar was exciting, a trip Beyond our little town.

Another memory picture I have of her is at the 'surprise' birthday parties Dorothy gave me every year. On their dining table was a cake with candles, and a present with ribbon Mrs. V. had curled. I felt very special. To this day I never curl ribbon but what I think of Dorothy's mother with a warm glow.

My family moved to West Linn in 1956 when I was eleven but our friendship continued. Dorothy came with us on our trips to the Oregon coast and some summers I lived in woodsy campgrounds with the V. family while Mr. V. built roads in Estacada, Oregon, Carson, Washington, and Lakeside by Shasta in California. When we returned to their trailer from our daily rambles there was always dinner ready. I didn't appreciate that then, just expected it.

She smiled proudly at our grade school graduations and later, held our babies. Now it's April, Spring of 2013. Mrs. V. still lives in Gladstone. We exchange Christmas cards and messages every year. She's known for some time where that missing fudge pan went. Widowed now, she's pushed ninety out of the way and is moving on. It's long past time to say, "Thank you, Dottie, for the care you gave us. For that bedroom with a bookcase. For always welcoming the little girl up the street who wouldn't go home until you said it was time. For the example of a peaceful home. For trusting us to do our best. For loving us." Long past, but I've not forgotten.

Love, Patsy

Allen Brookshire, clamming in Yaquina Bay, 2011

This Is Now

Clamming in Yaquina Bay, Oregon

This week has had several very low tides in Yaquina Bay, clamming tides. The water retreats to expose the clam beds. Cockles, gapers, butter clams, many others. As a child my family clammed in Longbeach, Washington, for razor clams. That's a fast action, spy a small hole in the sand, step between hole and sea, a squirt means a clam is there. Start digging with shovel. Fast. Wasn't sure I was up to that but the literature about cockles and butter clams makes it sound easy. Just walk out there and pick them up. Almost. I can get a combo of about 30 clams, if I'm lucky. Alluring to this old clam digger.

The operative word there is old. I'm not really old (not even 70 yet), but to be taking up clam digging again, let us say I'm out of practice. Day before I sat in my car by the bay and watched folks out there with their shovels and buckets. Couldn't stand it anymore. Went to Walmart Sporting and bought a shellfish license. $7.00. Stopped by South Beach Grocery and picked up a free tide table.

Wednesday, April 20, 2011, low tide is highlighted in gray, will be 2.1 at 8:44 a.m. Good. Not TOO early.

By 7:00 a.m. I'd showered and got ready, put on warm clothes and my rubber boots. They are one size too large so I'm not comfortable in them. Not sure of clothes except I must keep my ears covered in case of wind. Jacket had to have pockets for my cell phone and camera.

I ate some yogurt and took an apple and cheddar cheese, a bagel and small thermos of coffee. I go nowhere without some food, am diabetic to a small degree and do pay attention to blood sugar levels. All this before I'm even in the car. I broke my clam shovel last year (it was old, belonged to my parents and harkened back to clamming of 50 years ago), so all I have is a trowel and a gardener's hand rake. They will have to do. This is an exploring expedition, to see what I need and whether I can do it or not. I gathered my bucket and put all this stuff plus a towel in my bucket. The bucket has the name of the brand of kitty litter that it held before coming to this use. Not attractive. I am ignoring my lack of 'correct gear'. Making do with what I have.

At parking lot at Hatfield Marine Science Center I parked the car close to the trail and bay. While unloading my bucket I exchange morning greetings with a young couple and their about 6-year-old daughter. Booted, with shovels and buckets, they set out just ahead of me. I'm glad I won't be alone on the flats. Looks to be empty of people out there. Once I hit the sand I am trudging in the boots that flap just that little bit because of the extra size. When I hit wet sand they become harder to walk in. Each step has suck in it requiring leg and knee energy to lift. Not bad, just annoying. Perhaps I should have worn my tennies.

Or gone barefoot like the women I'd talked with last year who clam barefoot so they can feel the scallops just below the sand. Hmmm. Perhaps this summer. Temp now is in mid 40's, maybe warmer. Comfortable with no wind. As it is this morning. Sunny, cool. Now I remember the spacious feeling of being out beyond regular tidal area; my shoulders expand, I sniff the air. Faintly briny. I fill my lungs. To say it feels good is to minimize the pleasure. Just imagine a sunny morning on the bay, sand and sea all a'glimmer.

Seagulls hop about but from all the empty clamshells littering the sand, I'd say that in the main they've taken their breakfast and are just relaxing. Perhaps I should have come as the tide was going out, following the exposure, instead of waiting until it was at lowest ebb. First lesson. I can see where some digging has been done. At a pool I dip the bucket in for sea water for my clams, to keep them alive and expelling sand, like Grandma used to do.

One thing I note, the sand has streaks of oil, and the sheen is in the pools. This I've seen on the beach, too. Was not there when I was a child. Modern times.

I see divots and scoop at them with my hand rake. A couple of times I snag a clam with a white oval shell and put it in my bucket. Something though I don't remember them on the clam list, from the photos in the regulations guide that I got with my license (had to ask for it). The walking becomes more difficult in these boots the further out I go, because it's wetter, softer. The suck means that every step is a pull. I go close to the father of the family, ask him about my whitish clam shell, show it to him. "I think that's a baby gaper." He shows me a large one he's dug, about 4 or 5 inches long, with a healthy neck for digging. He got it with his shovel. The method appears similar to digging for razor clams. I admire the size of his clam! He says I must keep my baby clam, can't put them back.

While I am talking to him I am stationary and feel my feet sinking in the muck. I pull up my boot but my foot comes out. I step into the sandy muck. I grab my bucket for stability as I pull up my wet, socked foot and put it back in the boot. Yuck.

We talk clamming as I re-stabilize myself. A friendly guy, he tells me there are no razors here in the bay, they are on the beach. I express my disappointment about the cockles, had thought from reading I could just pick them up. "Usually the cockles are closer to the surface," he says. "Sometimes you can just pick them up. Not today though." I leave him to his work, aim for drier, firmer sand. Find more of the white clam shells, also start to collect empty shells, gotta have something for my time here.

Finding more of the whites I enter onto soft, wet sand again, and before I know it, I am unbalanced as my boot is sucked to stay in place, but my body tips. My arms flail about, nothing to hold on to. This time I sit (fall, slowly) down in the muck, my hands breaking the fall. I reach for the bucket, use it to lever up. The whole back of me wet, sandy. Feet stayed in boots though. Decide to pack it in. The walk back takes 15 minutes during which time I answer John's call on the cell, needs to be picked up at work. Now I find two cockles, yes, lying in shallow water in the sand. I got them before the gulls did (no gulls about, it is my private contest), and took some photos. Back at the car I shed everything to the back of the Chevy van, put a large towel on my car seat and sat there for a few minutes, drinking coffee and eating cheese on my bagel. I am tired. But happy.

Lessons learned today:

1. I need a clam shovel to get the gapers. A couple of them and we could have a good chowder. The shovel would be good leverage, too, like that third leg that we find handy as we add the years.

2. Next time, either barefoot or tennies, these boots are a hazard to me. And I'd like a nicer bucket. Just for the appearance of it. I am amazed at my shallowness! Clam bed couture.

3. Start earlier, follow the tide out, catch the clams unaware, before the gulls get them.

When I get home with John, I am exhausted from the exertion of pulling the boots from the suction of the sand. Still happy. I spread out my clams and shells on the picnic table in our backyard. Find that most of my white shells are full of sand. Have 3 clams, two cockles, one gaper. For dinner I steam them, happy to see them pop open, though I do feel just a tinge sad for them, (but gulls eat them alive!). I heat butter, add garlic salt, into which we dip the catch, for an appetizer. One for John, two for me. His first steamers. Exquisite, but think I should have given them another minute in the boiling water after they opened. Maybe. Will read up on it, while I save money for a real clam shovel and bucket to be ready for next low tides. Free food always costs, doesn't it. That is not a question, it's a state of life fact.

Today, Thursday, the day after, I awake with tiny aches in both knees, general feeling of ache, but all is okay. I am good to go.

Thanks for listening. Cheerio.

April 21, 2011

Prince Charming in the snow at Peaceable Kingdom

The Peaceable Kingdom Turns White

Early this morning we woke deep in the back of the cave. Brrr cold. I crawled from under the furs and over to the fire. It had gone out. John made his way in the dark to his news machine. He was expecting to work driving today. I worked my way around the cave, getting coffee 'perking' and telling Miz Bella, our sweet kitty, "No, you can't go out into the forest. Too dark and a critter might be waiting to grab you," when John called out. "It's not snowing, is it?"

"No. Certainly not." Then I went to the front of the cave with a candle … and looked out. Oh, my. The groundhog was right. "The porch is covered with snow!" I flashed with excitement. Might 'school' be closed today?!

Motivated, I got birdseed ready, heated up hot water to melt the ice in the outside water bowls, and checked our supply of yeast. Good, two packets. Then to the lower part of the cave to get kindling. We have a goodly supply from brother Al this past summer.

Once I had the fire blazing, the dawn light revealed the outline of trees, the birdbath, the car, Al's twig trellis, and our Christmas tree that is sitting on the front lawn in its holder. All covered with the white stuff. More coming down. Outside the cave sit the two bird feeders.

I wrapped up in my Alaska coat and non-slip shoes and looked out the back of the cave. Fast falling and blowy snow, just like in front. I trudged through the slippery stuff and filled the feeders, plus hung up two suet packets. Miz Bella took a look outside, tested that white frosting with a tentative paw and jumped back into the cave.

She and I watched from the viewing port as the birds flocked to the seed. The ground and feeders were covered with redwing blackbirds, a couple stray starlings, a lovely orange breasted varied thrush. Two gray doves and a yellow eyebrow sparrow (my name for a bird I don't know the name of..) contested with the Steller's Jays for seeds on the ground. Into our view flew my favorite, the little song sparrows, with popcorn-design chests, that hop around fetchingly.

John made us breakfast of ham and eggs then mushed the sled into town to get money to pay the wood guy (he likes cash). He'd called earlier wanting to know if instead of this weekend we'd like our cord delivered today. Would we! Elated at the surplus of wood we would be having, I sprung the yeast from our two packets into a bit of sugar and warm water, and mixed up a batch of raisin bread. Covered with a clean old kitchen towel, it fit on the hearth between the wood stove and the wood box.

But then the wood guy called to say the world was turning bad at his house. Couldn't come. Freezing ice. "Freezing ice?" I whined, thinking, come on, just tough it out, you can make it. "You know what freezing ice is, don't you?" he said. I snarled, "Don't get snotty with me!" "Okay," he said, his tone careful as if he had just bumped into a crazy person. I had to call back and apologize. We'll be okay, it's just that in my flurry of happiness at the excess wood we would have I'd been burning our last pieces with abandon. Truly, we have enough, I was just going through a bad patch of fear of freezing.

The cave is warmed, birds are fed, Miz Bella happy to play with her catnip mouse or doze on the couch in front of the fire, and John has dinner ready. The groundhog is our friend. How goes it at your house?

February 6, 2014

Listing of Poems and Prose
With Dates Written

About the Author

Patsy Brookshire has lived on the Oregon coast since 1980. She loves the rain, the mist and, yes, the sea lions basking on the docks, scrabbling with each other for space in the sun. Patsy can relate. Her husband, John Port, passed in 2014. Her friends, children and brother, Allen, help her battle raccoons while accommodating house cats and the varied birds and waterfowl living on the adjacent wetland. She is, she reports, living the good life.

Ruby Rose is Patsy's alternate personality, the one responsible for anything quirky or fanciful.

Patsy is the author of the *Sophie's Kin and Quilt Suspense Series*, available from Amazon.com and other bookstores. Also e-published by Uncial Press. Order at uncialpress.com.

Patsy loves to hear from her readers. She can be contacted via e-mail: brookport@peak.org
or PO Box 1805, Newport, OR 97365

###

Made in the USA
Middletown, DE
18 August 2022

70784035R00106